MEXICO
the culture

Bobbie Kalman

The Lands, Peoples, and Cultures Series

Crabtree Publishing Company

The Lands, Peoples, and Cultures Series

Created by Bobbie Kalman

For Judy and Norman Reiach and Edwin Deal, who brought me to Nassau

Editor-in-Chief
Bobbie Kalman

Writing team
Bobbie Kalman
Tammy Everts

Editors
David Schimpky
Janine Schaub
Lynda Hale
Tammy Everts

Computer design and layout
Lynda Hale
Antoinette "Cookie" DeBiasi

Printer
Worzalla Publishing Company

Separations and film
Book Art Inc.

Special thanks to: Jürgen Bavoni, Danny Brauer, Monique Denis, DeYoung Museum, Library of Congress, Mexican Government Tourism Office, Marla Misunas, and Laurie Taylor

Photographs

Jürgen Bavoni: pages 4, 12 (top), 15, 21-23 (all), 25 (top right and oval), 26 (top left)
Jim Bryant: pages 3, 6, 7 (top), 9 (top left and right), 11 (top), 12 (middle), 26 (bottom left, bottom right), 28-29
Richard Emblin: title page
Fowler Museum of Cultural History, UCLA: page 12 (bottom)
Bobbie Kalman: cover, pages 14, 16, 17 (all), 26 (top right)
Diane Payton Majumdar: pages 7 (bottom), 25 (bottom)
Mexican Government Tourism Office: page 11 (bottom)
Jean Robertson: page 10
San Francisco Museum of Modern Art: page 13 *Frieda and Diego Rivera*, 1931, by Frida Kahlo; oil on canvas, 100.01 x 78.75 cm (39 3/8 x 31 inches) Albert M. Bender Collection, Gift of Albert M. Bender
Superstock/Steve Vidler: page 5

Illustrations

Antoinette "Cookie" DeBiasi: pages 8 (top), 9, 19, 29, 30, back cover
Tammy Everts: page 8 (middle, bottom), 28
Lisa Smith: page 20

Published by
Crabtree Publishing Company

350 Fifth Avenue
Suite 3308
New York
N.Y. 10118

360 York Road, RR 4,
Niagara-on-the-Lake,
Ontario, Canada
L0S 1J0

73 Lime Walk
Headington
Oxford OX3 7AD
United Kingdom

Cataloguing in Publication Data

Kalman, Bobbie, 1947-
  Mexico: the culture

(Lands, Peoples, and Cultures Series)
Includes index.
ISBN 0-86505-216-6 (library bound) ISBN 0-86505-296-4 (pbk.)
This book looks at the ancient and modern culture of Mexico, including art, music, dance, and festivals.

1. Mexico - Social life and customs - Juvenile literature.
2. Mexico - Civilization - Juvenile literature. I. Title. II. Series.

F1210.K35 1993   j972

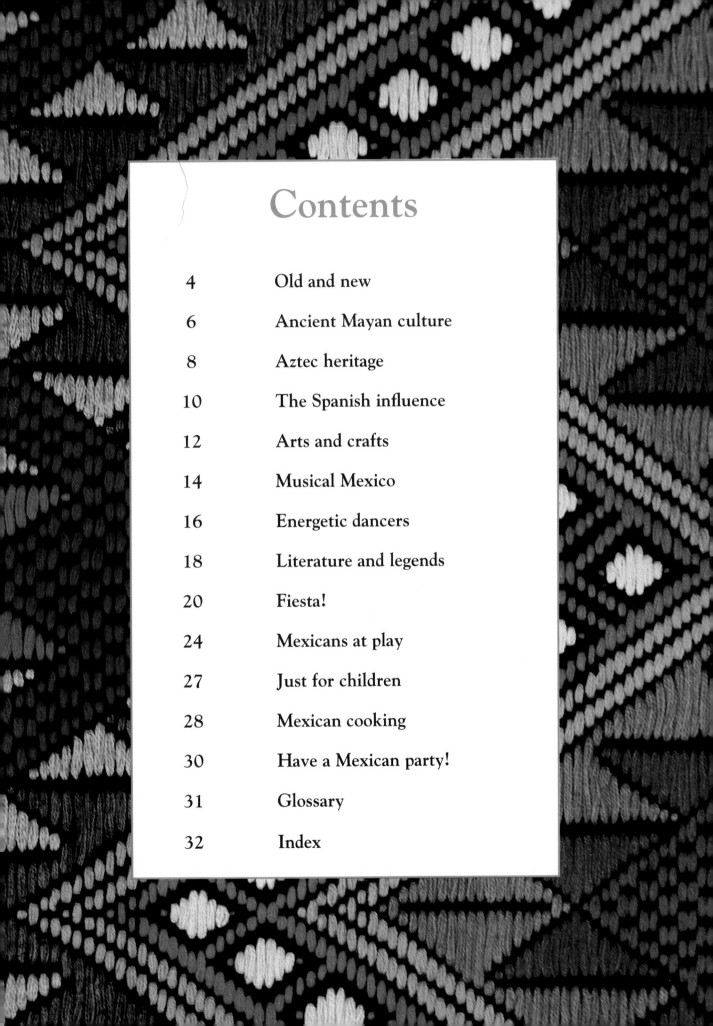

Contents

Culture is the way people dress, the food they eat, the music they play, the buildings they construct, and the art they create. It includes dancing, singing, performing, and celebrating. Culture represents traditions from the past and more recent customs. Mexico's lively culture is a blend of old and new.

Back to pyramid times

The culture of Mexico is very old. It goes back to a time when Native peoples built pyramids in the rainforest thousands of years ago. The Native peoples of Mexico had very advanced societies. They were called **civilizations** because they were more advanced than the societies of many other peoples around the world. Ancient Mexican civilizations included the Olmecs, Zapotecs, Maya, and Aztecs. Traces of their writings, mathematical skills, remarkable buildings, and religions are still evident in Mexico today.

More recent influences

The culture of Mexico has also been influenced by the Spanish, who sailed over from Europe and ruled the people of Mexico for many years. Mexico's neighbor, the United States, has contributed as well to the modern culture of Mexico through television programs, movies, music, and fashions. In fact, the millions of tourists from all over the world who visit Mexico each year leave behind a little of their cultures.

Colorful and lively

Mexican culture is made up of the customs and traditions of many peoples. That is probably why it is so colorful and lively. Happy fiestas, exciting bullfights, energetic dances, elaborate murals, mysterious ruins, and friendly people are all part of Mexico's culture. Mexicans love life. *Olé!*

Ancient Mayan culture

From 400 BC to AD 900 the Maya were the most powerful people in Mexico. From the information that remains about this ancient culture, we know that the Maya were very skillful. They were experts at mathematics and astronomy. They also built many awesome structures.

Books and writing

The Maya developed one of the first writing systems in North America. Mayan **hieroglyphs**, or **glyphs**, used pictures or symbols to represent words and ideas. Glyphs were written on walls and in books.

Mayan books, called **codices**, did not have pages as modern books do. Instead, they were pleated and had to be unfolded in order to be read. Each codex told stories about the Mayan gods and important people. Only three codices remain. The rest were destroyed by the Spanish, who came to Mexico almost 500 years ago.

Murals

The Maya also left behind large **murals**, or wall paintings, showing royal ceremonies. The best examples of Mayan murals can be seen at the ancient city of Bonampak. They demonstrate the great talent of the ancient Maya for creating dazzling shades of paint. One such color, called Maya Blue, was envied by other Native cultures. Try as they might, they could not reproduce it.

Many different gods

Religion was a very important part of Mayan life. The Maya believed that each part of the world was ruled by a different god. The gods could bring health, good crops, and plentiful food to the people, or they could send illness and hunger. Peasant farmers prayed to a rain god named Chac and to a *maize* god called Yum Kaax. Prayers and offerings of food were used to keep the gods happy.

Pyramids and palaces

The Mayan civilization is famous for its elaborate buildings, which demanded great engineering skill. These buildings were not made of wood or stone; they were constructed from concrete, which is still an important building material used today.

The Maya built pyramids that were sometimes 60 meters (200 feet) high! The pyramids were monuments to Mayan gods and leaders. Unlike the pointed pyramids of the ancient Egyptians, Mayan temples had flat tops upon which the rulers sat.

Mayan palaces were built differently than the pyramids. They were not as tall, and they held many more rooms. The pyramids and palaces were often arranged around large courts or gardens, forming small cities. Some of these cities are still standing.

Many people visit the ancient site of Chichén Itzá each year. Most of this city was built by the Maya, although some buildings are believed to be the work of the Toltecs, who were later inhabitants of the city. It includes many solid stone structures, such as the Castle (opposite page), the Temple of the Warriors, and the Complex of 1000 Columns (above).
(left) Statues of Mayan gods have been uncovered all across southern Mexico. Most have serious expressions on their faces, as this statue does. The elaborate headdress identifies the importance of the god.

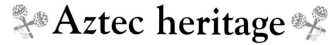

Aztec heritage
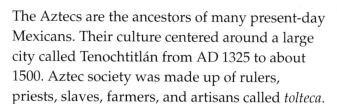

The Aztecs are the ancestors of many present-day Mexicans. Their culture centered around a large city called Tenochtitlán from AD 1325 to about 1500. Aztec society was made up of rulers, priests, slaves, farmers, and artisans called *tolteca*.

An artistic society

The Aztecs felt that creativity was very important, so the *tolteca* were highly respected. They lived in a separate part of the city. Artisans passed their skills on to their children and grandchildren. As a result, huge families of *tolteca* all practiced the same craft. These crafts included working with gold, silver, turquoise, shells, feathers, wood, and stone.

The Aztecs also appreciated the arts of other cultures. They brought many Mayan, Zapotec, and Mixtec artists to Tenochtitlán—sometimes against their will! From these peoples, the Aztecs learned the arts of tie-dying, batiking, feather-working, and embroidery.

caterpillar

mountain

teeth

gold

Tenochtitlán

Montezuma II

(top left) Ceremonial costumes were made using fur and hundreds of colorful feathers. (above and left) Like the Maya, the Aztecs used hieroglyphs. Pictured here are some of the symbols used for Aztec words and ideas. (below) The Aztecs also had codices. Most were destroyed by the Spanish.

(above) Fearsome faces scowl at visitors to the Temple of Quetzalcoatl, which honored a powerful Aztec god. (left) The Aztec **volador** ceremony is still practiced in some regions of Mexico. Four men, dressed as gods in bird form, jump from a revolving platform atop a tall pole. As the ropes that are attached to their feet unwind, the men fly around the pole thirteen times, the number of days in a religious calendar week.

The Aztec calendar

Like the Maya, the Aztecs were astronomers and mathematicians. They developed two **calendars** that were based on the movements of the sun and stars. A calendar is a way of dividing the year into months, weeks, and days. The **solar calendar**, which was based on the sun, was divided into 365 days. It had eighteen months with twenty days in each month. The five leftover days were considered unlucky. The **religious calendar** divided the year into 260 days, with twenty weeks of thirteen days each.

Aztec calendars looked very different from the calendars we use today. The huge Aztec Calendar Stone stood in the Great Temple in Tenochtitlán. This brightly painted, flat, round stone showed the Sun God surrounded by symbols that represented the stars and planets. It was used by Aztec priests to remember religious holidays and predict **solar eclipses**. A solar eclipse occurs when the moon is directly between the earth and the sun. From the earth, it appears that only a small ring of sunlight is left to shine around the moon's edges. The Aztecs believed that eclipses were messages from the gods, so they were careful to remember when a solar eclipse would occur.

The Spanish influence

When the Spanish conquered the Native peoples, they also destroyed much of the art and architecture of Mexico. The Aztec city of Tenochtitlán was torn down, and the modern capital Mexico City was built on its ruins. The Spanish had a strong influence on Mexico's culture.

Spanish language

One of the biggest changes made by the Spaniards was the change of language. Dozens of Native languages had been spoken in Mexico, but the Spaniards made the Mexican Natives learn to speak Spanish. Today some Native tongues are still spoken in rural areas, but Spanish is the national language of Mexico.

Christianity

Spanish priests converted the Native peoples to Christianity. The Natives were too afraid to resist. Today almost every Mexican is Roman Catholic. Native ways still remain, but they have blended with Roman-Catholic traditions. For example, ancient Native dances are performed to celebrate Catholic holidays.

Graceful architecture

The Spanish built hundreds of Catholic churches in Mexico. These buildings are majestic and beautiful. The town of San Miguel de Allende is proud of its handsome Spanish colonial architecture. It is one of three villages in Mexico that have been declared national monuments.

This means that it is illegal for any of the buildings, with their graceful arches and spires, to be torn down or for any new buildings to be erected.

Decorating with gold

The Spanish conquerors were fascinated by the numerous golden objects they saw in Tenochtitlán. Hungry for more gold, they enslaved the Native Mexicans and forced them to work under terrible conditions in gold mines. Many died while mining the gold, which the Spaniards used for making jewelry, statues, and church decorations.

(opposite page) The National University of Mexico was founded by the Spanish in 1551. It is the oldest university in North America!
(right) Detailed carvings and statues can be found on many Spanish colonial churches, such as the magnificent Church of San Francisco in Tepotzotlán.
(bottom) Beautiful Catholic churches can be seen throughout Mexico.

🪓 Arts and crafts 🪓

Folk art

Mexicans have been creating beautiful handmade crafts for thousands of years. Today many Mexican villages carry on the ancient traditions of the Aztec *tolteca*. The silversmiths of Taxco are world famous for their jewelry, whereas the craftsworkers of Talavera are well known for their terra-cotta pottery. Artists in Jalisco have a reputation for making beautiful hand-blown glassware. Several villages in the Oaxacan Valley specialize in painting wooden carvings of animals, people, and strange creatures.

Murals

Hundreds of years ago the Maya painted colorful murals showing scenes of wealthy people enjoying life. The tradition of painting murals is still popular in Mexico, but modern murals present different themes, such as poverty and suffering. The most famous modern muralists are known as "The Big Three." Their names are Diego Rivera, José Clemente Orozco, and David Alfaro Siqueiros.

Become a Mexican potter

You can make your own Mexican art. Brightly painted Mexican pottery is popular in many countries. Create your own custom-designed pot for holding plants, marbles, or pens. Buy a clay or terra-cotta pot (a flowerpot will do). Use enamel paint to decorate the outside of the pot. Mexican art uses wild colors and bold designs. Look at the picture of this pot and then come up with a design of your own.

Create your own mural

Decorate a classroom wall with a Mexican-style mural. Decide on a scene, such as a crowded schoolyard or a jungle filled with wildlife, and draw a detailed sketch on paper. Draw a grid over your sketch, then draw a much larger matching grid on the background on which you will paint. Each student can work on transferring a block of the sketch to the matching block on the wall. Make sure that everyone's parts fit together!

(above) Frida Kahlo, the wife of Diego Rivera, painted in a simple style called **primitivism**. *Kahlo's paintings are collected by art lovers around the world. This painting shows her wedding day.*
(opposite page, top) Papier-mâché folk art is a popular souvenir for visitors from other countries.
(opposite page, middle) Diego Rivera's murals sympathized with the problems faced by Mexican Native peoples.

 # Musical Mexico

Like people everywhere, Mexicans listen to all kinds of music—from rock to traditional to classical. There are eight major symphony orchestras in Mexico. Traditional Mexican music is still played by *mariachis* and *norteños*. Some Mexican folk songs have been around for hundreds of years, such as the popular song *La Cucaracha*, which means "the cockroach" in Spanish. In village plazas, musicians play on traditional xylophone-like instruments called *marimbas*.

Norteños

Norteños, or *rancheros* as they are sometimes called, are not well known outside Mexico, but they are very popular within the country. *Norteño* groups have three musicians: an accordian player, a guitarist, and a singer who also plays on a piece of wood with drumsticks. *Norteño* music sounds like country-and-western music.

Mariachis

For many people, *mariachi* bands are a symbol of Mexico. These groups of six to eight musicians wander about plazas and in and out of restaurants and taverns, playing songs for a fee. An average *mariachi* band has a singer, two violinists, two guitarists, two horn players, and a bass player. All of them dress in sparkling uniforms and wide-brimmed hats. Some people believe that *mariachis* date from the short time

that the French army occupied Mexico. Many French soldiers married Mexican women, and they hired small bands to play at their weddings. The bands were later called *mariachis*, from the French word for marriage (*mariage*). They became popular at all kinds of celebrations.

María Grever

Mexico's favorite songwriter is a woman named María Grever. Grever wrote 873 popular songs in her lifetime! Many of these songs were inspired by ancient Mexican folk songs. Grever was awarded the Civil Merit Medal for her cultural gift to the Mexican people.

Carlos Chávez

Carlos Chávez's powerful music has made him the most famous classical composer in the history of Mexico. In 1917 Chávez wrote his first symphony at the age of eighteen! During his long musical career, Chávez worked as a conductor, teacher, and director. He is responsible for the creation of the National Opera of Mexico. His goal was to remind people of the beauty of ancient Native music.

(above) **Mariachis** *stroll through city streets looking for someone who needs some cheerful music.*
(opposite page) *Three young trumpeters practice their instruments. Perhaps they would like to be* **mariachis** *when they grow up.*

Energetic dancers

Dance is a very important part of Mexican culture. Mexicans feel that it keeps them in touch with their Native heritage. Ancient dances are performed in traditional costumes. Modern performers base their steps on the movements of centuries-old dances.

Dance of the Little Old Men

The *danza de los viejitos*, or "Dance of the Little Old Men," is one of the oldest dances in Mexico. Young men are made up to look like toothless, wrinkled old men. The dancers hobble around with walking sticks until suddenly they leap up and start dancing energetically. Just as quickly, they become weak old men again until another burst of energy hits them. These antics cause the audience to erupt in gales of laughter.

Traveling dancers

Conchero dancers often perform at Mexican holidays called **fiestas**. Men and women dance ancient Native dances to the music of a guitar or lute. Their colorful costumes include tall, plumed headdresses, wide capes, sequined robes, embroidered shields, and clusters of bells and dried shells at the ankles. *Conchero* dancers travel from fiesta to fiesta, dancing for hours without getting tired.

Dances with swords

Matachin sword dancers are also popular at fiestas, delighting both children and adults. The dancers wear tall, pointed headdresses and cover part of their faces with a fringe. Dressed in layers of aprons and multicolored ribbons, the dancers shake gourd rattles in one hand and wield brightly painted wooden swords in the other.

Ballet

The Ballet Folklórico was formed by Mexican dancer Amália Hernández in 1952. Today the Folklórico has three different troupes of dancers. Two of them tour the world, and the third performs at the Palace of Fine Arts in Mexico City. The Folklórico performances combine modern dance techniques with traditional Native costumes and music. Ballets are based on ancient stories of the gods and emperors. The colorful costumes and lively dance routines have gained fame at home and around the world.

Mexican Hat Dance

The *jarabe tapatío*, or Mexican Hat Dance, is the national dance of Mexico. Male dancers wear a rodeo-rider costume called a *charro*, and the women wear brightly colored full skirts that swirl around them as they move. The performers dance with quick hopping steps around a wide-brimmed Mexican hat called a **sombrero**.

Kick up your heels!

You can learn an easy version of the Mexican Hat Dance from a teacher, parent, or neighbor. This simple version was once popular at parties, and most adults know how to do it. You hop from heel to heel, clap your hands, and promenade as you would in a square dance, linking arms with all the other dancers as you meet them.

Mexican dancers perform at fiestas, tourist hotels, and night clubs. One of the most energetic dances is the Rooster and Hen dance (opposite page, top right). The Mexican Hat Dance (bottom left) is a favorite with Mexicans and tourists.

Literature and legends

The first printing press in North America was used in Mexico City in 1539! Today, writing is still Mexico's greatest contribution to world culture. Book, newspaper, and magazine publishing are among the biggest industries in Mexico.

Literature old and new

One of Mexico's earliest poets was a seventeenth-century nun named Sister Juana Inès de la Cruz. Her poetry is considered among the finest ever written in the Spanish language. Octavio Paz is a popular modern Mexican poet who has written a great deal about Mexican life. Rosario Castellanos writes poems about the Native peoples of the state of Chiapas and the changing role of women in Mexican society. Juan Rulfo and Carlos Fuentes are two well-known Mexican novelists. Nobel prize-winning author Gabriel García Marquez also lives in Mexico.

Folk tales and legends

Mexican folk tales, or **myths**, spring from several sources. Some come from the Mayan people, some from the Aztecs, and others are a combination of many Native cultures. The following legend tells the story of the creation of the earth. It explains how people came to be and why some are poor and others are wealthy.

Golden Man and the Finger People

Many years ago, the gods created the world. They covered its surface with mountains, plains, oceans, and rivers. They made animals to live on the land and fish to swim in the water. Though they had created so much, the gods still felt that something was missing. The earth was beautiful, but there was no one to praise the work of the gods. The gods needed a new being to whom they could give the gifts of life, language, and reason. They set to work creating such a creature. The first one was made of clay. The gods tested its strength by throwing it in the water. The clay creature turned to mud and disappeared.

The gods were filled with despair, but they tried again, this time creating a being of wood. The wooden creature floated in the water but, when the gods tested it with fire, it burned until nothing was left but ashes.

Again the gods were saddened, and they decided to make their next creature of gold, but there was only enough gold to make one being. The golden creature did not dissolve in the water or burn in the fire, so the gods gave him life, language, and reason.

The Golden Man was alive, but he was lonely. There was no one with whom he could share his ideas and feelings. Instead of praising the gods, he was angry and yelled at them. They had given him a body of gold and the knowledge of riches, but no one with whom he could share his gifts.

The gods were filled with sorrow when they heard the Golden Man's curses. One god was so upset that he dropped his sword, cutting off four of his fingers. As the fingers fell from the sky to the earth, the gods all cried out that the fingers should become the grateful creatures the gods had tried so hard to make. The falling fingers became people made of flesh, blood, and bones.

As they moved about the earth, the Finger People wondered at everything they saw. When they were thirsty, they drank with cupped hands from the river. Seeing the Golden Man nearby, they offered him some water, and he drank. They became friends, and the Golden Man shared with them his knowledge of riches. They all rejoiced in their lives and thanked the gods for their happiness. The gods were finally content.

From that day forward, the gods decided that there would always be wealthy people and those who are less fortunate so that they could learn from one another and from the world around them.

Fiesta!

In Mexico there are 365 main fiesta days—
a holiday for every day of the year! Fiesta
means "feast day" in Spanish, but feasts are
only one part of these Mexican celebrations.
Religious festivals, parades, fireworks, music,
and dancing are other favorite ways of rejoicing.

Many reasons to celebrate

Celebrations are not limited to feast days.
Weddings, graduations, birthdays, baptisms,
First Communions, and confirmations are also
festive occasions. On these days, Mexicans hire a
mariachi band, send flowers, and invite friends
and family to help celebrate. Fiestas are also held
to celebrate visitors to Mexico and allow them
to sample Mexico's rich culture.

Day of Our Lady of Guadalupe

The largest and most popular ceremony is the
fiesta celebrating the Virgin of Guadalupe.
Mary, the mother of Jesus, appeared in a vision
to a Native Mexican many years ago. Every year
on December 12, over six million Mexicans and
people from other countries travel to her shrine,
called La Villa, in Mexico City.

On this day, Mexicans rise early and gather in
the village plaza, where they are met by flags,
balloons, bands, and dancing. After dark, a
bamboo *castillo*, or castle, is brightly lit by
spectacular fireworks that explode and show the
outlines of birds and flowers. No one would ever
think of going home until the fireworks are over.

Christmas

Christmas is one of the favorite holidays of Mexican children, perhaps because it lasts more than one week! The celebration begins on December 16 with a *posada*, a play about Mary and Joseph's journey into Bethlehem. *Posadas* are performed every evening until December 25. After each *posada*, there is great excitement as the children gather around a *piñata* filled with toys and candy. Wearing blindfolds, they try to break it open with a stick.

Mexican families are very proud of the nativity scenes that they put up in their homes. These scenes, called *nacimientos*, or birthplaces, contain beautifully crafted wax statues.

Celebrating the Three Wise Men

Mexican children do not receive presents on Christmas Day, but this does not bother them. They know that gift-giving occurs on January 6, the day on which Mexicans celebrate the arrival of the Three Wise Men at the birthplace of Jesus. On this day, Mexican bakers busily prepare La Rosca de los Reyes, or the Ring of the Wise Men, a delicious circular cake with a tiny porcelain doll mixed in with the dough. The little doll represents the gifts the Wise Men gave to baby Jesus. It is a surprise for the person who finds it.

Easter

Chocolate bunnies and decorated eggs are not a part of Mexican children's Easter. Feasting, dancing, and merrymaking are ways in which Mexicans celebrate the resurrection of Jesus Christ. On the Saturday before Easter, a very popular Mexican custom called "the Burning of Judas" takes place. In the past, **effigies**, or life-sized dolls, of Judas were burned. Judas Iscariot was the disciple who betrayed Jesus. Today, Mexicans burn effigies of the politicians they dislike.

(top) Young girls dressed in white from head to toe participate in an Easter parade.
(bottom) Three young boys act out the journey of the the Wise Men to Bethlehem.

All Saints' Day

November 1 is All Saints' Day—a time when Mexican families honor their dead relatives. This religious celebration may sound very sad, but it is actually a joyful occasion. Many Mexicans believe that the spirits of their dead family members visit their homes in the early hours of All Saints' Day. In order to welcome these friendly ghosts, families leave presents or treats for them.

Later that day, everyone goes to the cemetery and decorates family graves with flowers before enjoying a picnic nearby. The picnic is believed to make the spirits feel welcome and happy if they decide to visit their graves. At night, candles are lit at each grave to help the spirits find their resting places in the darkness.

(opposite page) A mock wedding for skeletons is a fun part of Day of the Dead celebrations. (below) Two boys camp out by a relative's grave on the evening of All Saints' Day.

The Day of the Dead

The day after All Saints' Day is the Day of the Dead—a day of festivity. Mexican children look forward to eating candies and suckers in the shape of human skulls. Mexican bakers try to outdo one another by baking the most delicious coffee cake called Pan de los Muertos, or Bread of the Dead.

(circle) Offerings of flowers and gifts make the ghosts of dead relatives feel welcome.

Mexicans at play

In their spare time, Mexicans like to swim, jog, fish, and play games. Some sports, such as soccer and baseball, were imported from other countries. Bullfighting and *jai alai* were introduced to Mexico by the Spanish.

Fútbol

Fútbol, which is actually soccer, is the most popular sport in Mexico. The country has a professional soccer league in which dozens of teams compete. The World Cup Games, the most important soccer championship in the world, take place every four years. When Mexico competes in the Games, everyone watches television or listens to the radio, praying that their team will win. Important games are played in the Azteca Stadium in Mexico City. This huge stadium can hold up to 100,000 people!

Béisbol

Béisbol, or baseball, is almost as popular as soccer. It was introduced to Mexico by the United States over fifty years ago. Since then, many famous baseball players have come from Mexico, including Bobby Avila, who played with the Cleveland Indians in the 1950s. He is a national hero. After he retired from baseball, he became an important politician.

Jai alai

Jai alai, or *pelota*, is a fast-paced Spanish game played with a hard rubber ball and a wicker bat called a *cesta*, which is tied to the player's wrist. *Jai alai* is a little bit like tennis, but it is much faster. Some people call it the fastest ball game in the world because the ball can travel up to 260 kilometers (160 miles) per hour!

Rodeos

Most Mexican towns have a rodeo ring where riders called *charros* perform tricks on horseback and rope bulls with lassoes. These lively rodeos, called *charreodas*, are followed by lively parties.

The bullfighting tradition

The Spanish conquerors brought bullfighting to Mexico in the sixteenth century. It is still a popular spectator sport, especially for visitors. There are over 220 bullrings in Mexico, where bullfighting takes place from November to April. The Plaza de Mexico bullring, located in Mexico City, is the largest in the world.

Matadors

Expert bullfighters are called **matadors**. Being a matador is dangerous—one in four is crippled and one in ten is killed during a bullfight. Watching a talented matador in the ring is like observing a dancer performing an elaborate dance. The best matadors are greatly admired for their bravery and are considered heroes. When a matador kills a bull honorably, the cry "*Olé!*" rings through the bullring.

The suit of lights

Many young Mexican boys wish to be matadors so that they, too, can wear the spectacular "suit of lights." The matador's costume is a skin-tight suit studded with silver and gold disks that shimmer in the sunlight. A small hat tops off the outfit. While the matador is fighting the bull, he flourishes a bright red cape that is draped over his shoulders. It was once believed that the color red makes bulls angry, but bulls are colorblind. It is the movement of the cape that agitates the bulls.

Cruelty to animals?

Some Mexicans and people from other countries think that bullfighting is cruel because so many bulls are killed. This tradition was banned twice in Mexico, but it returned each time. Most Mexicans consider bullfighting an important part of their culture and believe that it is no more cruel than killing other animals for their meat.

(circle) **Fútbol** *is popular among Mexicans young and old.*
(right) *This young boy proudly shows off the tight costume and wide-brimmed sombrero of the* **charro**.
(bottom) *Bullfighting is a dangerous sport that draws thousands of visitors to Mexico each year.*

Mexican children enjoy many of the same games, activities, television shows, and musical groups that you do. Whether they live in the city or country, fun is an important part of every child's life!

Handball

Balonmano, or handball, is one of the world's oldest pastimes. It is especially popular among Mexican boys and girls. The Maya of ancient Mexico had handball courts that can still be seen in the midst of ancient ruins. Their version of handball was not just a game but a religious ceremony. The ball represented the sun, which was considered a powerful god. If a person was unlucky enough to drop the ball, he or she had to die. Today, handball is less dangerous to one's health. It is played just for fun!

Handclapping rhymes

Like children around the world, Mexican young people have rhymes that they sing while clapping their hands in complicated patterns. This Mexican handclapping rhyme, or *palmada*, is one that you can learn in Spanish or English:

Un elefante	One elephant
Se columpiaba	Went out one day
Sobre la tela	On a spider's web.
De una araña.	When he saw
Como vera que resistia	He didn't fall
Fue a llamar a	He went and called
Otro elefante.	Another elephant.
Dos elefantes . . .	Two elephants . . .
Tres elefantes . . .	Three elephants . . .

Rock music

Many young Mexicans love rock music. Every year there are several big rock concerts in Mexico City. A popular group called Menudo comes from Mexico. It is made up of five young Mexican boys. When one of them reaches the age of fourteen, a new boy auditions for his part, so the members of Menudo always stay young.

Day of Saint Anthony the Abbot

January 17 is a special day for Mexican children—and for their pets, too! On this day, which honors the saint who loved children and animals, young people wash and brush their pets and sometimes even dress them in decorated collars and fancy hats! In the morning the children and animals form a long line and parade through the town and into the churchyard, where the parish priest waits to bless the animals one by one. In the city, boys and girls bring cats, dogs, turtles, or goldfish, whereas country children bring chickens, ducks, sheep, or burros. No animal is too big or too small to be blessed!

Happy birthday!

Birthdays are a big event in many countries, and it is no different in Mexico. In some cases, the birthday begins very early in the morning, as the birthday boy or girl is awoken by a *mariachi* band right outside his or her bedroom window! Birthday parties are fun-filled occasions. Family and friends gather in the house or the park for an afternoon of food and games. The highlight of the party is breaking open the *piñata* after dinner. *Piñatas* sometimes come in traditional star or horse shapes, but modern birthday *piñatas* look like popular cartoon characters.

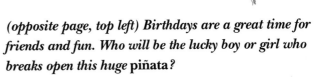

(opposite page, top left) Birthdays are a great time for friends and fun. Who will be the lucky boy or girl who breaks open this huge piñata?
(opposite page, top right) Like boys and girls around the world, young Mexicans enjoy caring for pets. This young girl loves her playful pet raccoon!
(opposite page, bottom left) Video games are a popular pastime of Mexican children.
(opposite page, bottom right) This Mexican boy teaches his younger brother how to ride a two-wheeled bike.

Mexican cooking

Mexican food is a flavorful mix of Spanish and Native cooking. Long before such foods as tomatoes, corn, avocadoes, vanilla, and cocoa were eaten in other parts of the world, cooks in ancient Mexico were using them in a wide variety of dishes. When the Spanish arrived in the 1500s, they introduced new foods, spices, and cooking techniques to the Natives. Pork, dairy products, and citrus fruits were quickly accepted into the Mexican diet. Today, Mexican food differs from region to region. In some areas it is hot and spicy; in others it is rich and sweet.

Making a Mexican meal

Invite your family to eat an authentic Mexican meal prepared by you! Making guacamole, tacos, Mexican hot chocolate, and *polvorones* is easy! Be sure to ask an adult for help when using a knife or the stove.

Guacamole

Guacamole is a favorite dip in some parts of Mexico. Serve guacamole with corn chips as an appetizer. Leftover guacamole can be stored in an airtight container in the refrigerator. Put the avocado pit in the middle of the dip—it helps keep the guacamole fresh!

2 ripe avocadoes
1/2 small onion
2 tomatoes
1 *jalapeño* pepper (optional)
30 ml (2 tablespoons) lemon juice
2-3 sprigs fresh cilantro (optional)
salt and pepper

Peel avocadoes and mash with fork. Place in bowl. Chop onion, cilantro, and pepper finely. Peel tomatoes and chop finely. Put all chopped ingredients in bowl. Add lemon juice, salt, and pepper to taste. Mix well. If you are not serving right away, cover bowl tightly with plastic wrap or foil, then refrigerate.

Tacos

Corn is the most important **staple food** in Mexico. A staple food is one that is eaten every day. Corn is very nutritious and is used in almost every dish: in tamales, enchiladas, and tortillas. Tacos are tortillas that are filled with a variety of vegetable, cheese, bean, or meat fillings. They are as popular in Mexico as hamburgers are in the United States. You can make them at home using this recipe.

450 g (1 lb) ground chicken or hamburger
5 ml (1 tsp) Mexican seasoning
5 ml (1 tsp) onion flakes
5 ml (1 tsp) dried cilantro
dash of cumin
dash of cayenne
12 taco shells
340 g (12 oz) shredded cheese
2 tomatoes
1 avocado
1 small head of lettuce

Brown meat in skillet. Drain excess grease. Add Mexican seasoning, onion flakes, cilantro, cumin, and cayenne. Cover and simmer for 10 minutes. Chop tomatoes and peeled avocado into small pieces. Shred the lettuce with hands or a knife. Place these toppings on separate plates. Heat taco shells in 150°C (300°F) oven for 5 minutes. Fill them with meat mixture. Top with tomatoes, avocado, lettuce, and cheese. This recipe makes 12 tacos.

Mexican hot chocolate

Long ago the Aztecs prepared a royal drink called *cacahel*, which was made with chocolate and chilies! The Spanish developed a new version of the drink by taking out the chilies and adding sugar and cinnamon. The result is a delicious frothy concoction that is easy to make.

60 ml (2 oz) unsweetened chocolate
500 ml (2 cups) milk
250 ml (1 cup) heavy cream
90 ml (6 tbsp) sugar
dash of cinnamon

Melt chocolate in the top of a double boiler. In a separate pot, warm milk and cream on low heat until hot but not boiling. Add a little hot milk to melted chocolate to form a paste. Stir in remaining milk, cream, sugar, and cinnamon. Serve immediately and enjoy!

Mexicans have a special tool called a *molinillo* with which they stir their hot chocolate. It is made of wood, has a number of round disks, and is rubbed between the hands. The spinning disks make the chocolate deliciously bubbly.

Polvorones

Polvorones are Mexican sugar cookies. They go well with hot chocolate.

500 ml (2 cups) flour
180 ml (3/4 cup) sugar
2.5 ml (1/2 tsp) cinnamon
250 ml (1 cup) butter or margarine
extra sugar and cinnamon

Preheat oven to 150°C (300°F). Sift together flour, cinnamon, and sugar. Cream butter with beater. Gradually add flour mixture. Pinch off small pieces of dough and shape into 24 patties. Place on ungreased cookie sheet. Bake for 25 minutes. Sprinkle extra sugar and cinnamon over warm cookies.

Have a Mexican party!

Have a party and make Mexico the theme! Ask guests to wear traditional Mexican costumes made of plain cotton pants and oversized shirts, white blouses and colorful skirts, and shawls and straw hats. Learn the Mexican Hat Dance, or make up a fun dance of your own! Prepare some of the Mexican recipes in this book. At the end of the party, have everyone try to break open a *piñata*. *Olé*!

How to make a *piñata*
You will need:
a large round balloon, inflated and tied
newspaper cut into long strips 3-5
    centimeters (1-2 inches) wide
flour and water paste (one part flour
    to two parts water)
8 sheets of different-colored tissue
    paper, each 50 by 75 centimeters
    (20 by 30 inches)
newspapers
masking tape
craft glue
3 meters (10 feet) heavy twine

Roll and cut five cones from three layers of newspaper. Each should be 18 centimeters (7 inches) long. Form the cones by overlapping the straight edges and gluing them together with craft glue.

Dip the newspaper strips in paste and apply four layers to the balloon, allowing layers to dry between applications. Leave 8 centimeters (3 inches) at stem end of balloon for opening.

Take the cones you have made and make cuts 3 centimeters (1 inch) deep around the base of each cone. Fold the cut edges back and paste them onto the wet *piñata*. Let the form dry completely. Deflate the balloon by snipping a hole in the exposed end. At this point, fill the *piñata* with candy or toys and put several coats of papier-mâché over the opening. Let it dry completely.

Attach the twine, circling the *piñata* from top to bottom in several loops. Use masking tape to hold the twine in place. Make a large loop at the top. Your *piñata* will hang from this loop, so make the knot a sturdy one.

Decorate the *piñata* with tissue-paper ruffles. Wild colors will make your *piñata* come alive! Using craft glue, paste the ruffles on in layers.

Make tassels for the cones by cutting different colors of tissue paper into thin strips. Divide the strips into five different bunches of mixed colored tissue. Glue or staple one bunch to each cone tip.

Glossary

agitate To provoke into a state of excitement

architecture The design and construction of buildings and structures

astronomy The study of the planets and stars

avocado A large green fruit with thick skin and a large pit

baptism A ceremony that shows that a person has become a Christian

bass A large violin-like instrument that plays low notes

batik A method of dying cloth to create interesting designs

burro A small donkey

cilantro Fresh coriander leaves

colonial Describing a land or people ruled by a distant country

colorblind The state of having a limited ability to distinguish between colors

communion A Christian ceremony that remembers the death of Jesus Christ

composer A person who writes original music

concrete Building material consisting of gravel or sand held together with mortar

conductor The person who directs an orchestra

confirmation A Christian ceremony in which a person renews his or her faith and is accepted into full membership of the church

custom A tradition practiced by many generations of people

embroidery The art of decorating cloth with needlework

fiesta A Mexican celebration

First Communion A Roman Catholic celebration that occurs when a child attends his or her first communion service

heritage Traditions and beliefs passed down by previous generations

jalapeño A spicy member of the pepper family

lasso A long rope with a loop at one end, used for roping cattle and horses

literature A body of creative written work

maize A Native word for corn

monument A structure that honors the memory of a person, idea, or event

myth A traditional story that tells the beliefs of a group of people

nativity scene A representation of the birthplace of Jesus Christ

Nobel Prize An international prize awarded for achievements in science, literature, and peace

novelist A person who writes long works of fiction called novels

nun A woman who has devoted her life to God

parish Describing or relating to an area with its own church

piñata A hollow, treat-filled papier-mâché figure broken during some Mexican celebrations

plaza An open area in the middle of a town or city

porcelain A hard white substance made by firing and glazing clay

pyramid A four-sided structure with a wide base and narrow top

rodeo A competition or demonstration of cowboy skills

Roman Catholic church The organization of Christians that is headed by the pope

saint A person recognized by a church for his or her goodness and service to the church

shrine A holy site dedicated to the worship of a religious figure

silversmith An artisan who works with silver

skillet A frying pan

spire The slender, pointed top of a church tower or steeple

symphony orchestra A large group of musicians who play classical music

terra cotta A hard clay used for pottery

tie-dye A method of dying cloth in which parts of the fabric are knotted, creating unusual color patterns

turquoise A valuable blue-green mineral

wicker A flexible tree shoot used for weaving baskets

xylophone A musical instrument featuring a row of wooden or metal bars which sound notes when tapped with a small hammer

 Index

1 2 3 4 5 6 7 8 9 0   Printed in U.S.A. 2 1 0 9 8 7 6 5 4 3